Once Upon A Dream

Cosmic Verse

Edited By Lynsey Evans

First published in Great Britain in 2024 by:

Young Writers
Remus House
Coltsfoot Drive
Peterborough
PE2 9BF
Telephone: 01733 890066
Website: www.youngwriters.co.uk

All Rights Reserved
Book Design by Ashley Janson
© Copyright Contributors 2024
Softback ISBN 978-1-83565-414-9
Printed and bound in the UK by BookPrintingUK
Website: www.bookprintinguk.com
YB0589H

FOREWORD

Welcome Reader, to a world of dreams.

For Young Writers' latest competition, we asked our writers to dig deep into their imagination and create a poem that paints a picture of what they dream of, whether it's a make-believe world full of wonder or their aspirations for the future.

The result is this collection of fantastic poetic verse that covers a whole host of different topics. Let your mind fly away with the fairies to explore the sweet joy of candy lands, join in with a game of fantasy football, or you may even catch a glimpse of a unicorn or another mythical creature. Beware though, because even dreamland has dark corners, so you may turn a page and walk into a nightmare!

Whereas the majority of our writers chose to stick to a free verse style, others gave themselves the challenge of other techniques such as acrostics and rhyming couplets.

Each piece in this collection shows the writers' dedication and imagination – we truly believe that seeing their work in print gives them a well-deserved boost of pride, and inspires them to keep writing, so we hope to see more of their work in the future!

CONTENTS

**Hob Green Primary School,
Pedmore Field**

Olivia Portman (9)	1
Daiton Hill (10)	2
Freya Jones (9)	3
Jasmine Taylor (9)	4
Eva Brazier (11)	5
Salma Kaid (10)	6
Zoyal Muqaddas (11)	7
Maddie Bowen (10)	8
Zaynab Quadoos (11)	9
Lyra Washington (11)	10
Leah Taylor (11)	11
Chase Rutherford (11)	12
Yaching Ko (7)	14
Rosie Fletcher (10)	15
Darcie-Rose Morgan (8)	16
Rowan Phipps (11)	17
Tiah Goodwin (10)	18
Ted Price (10)	19
Isaac Hammond (8)	20
Eva-Marie Withers (7)	21
Olivia Evans (10)	22
Symren Ahmedi (9)	23
Madison Pritchard (8)	24
Max Lewis Shilvock (8)	25
Evan Dowler (7)	26
Kai Toogood (11)	27
Imogen Lord (11)	28
Logan Campbell (8) & Musab	29
Jacob Clarke (11)	30
Mathew Roberts (11)	31
Hadi Israr (9)	32
Jenson Brazier (10)	33
Finley Bell (10)	34
Jacob Billingham (9)	35
Harvey Kerfoot (9)	36
Mia Turner (6)	37
Yahei Ko (9)	38
Liam Cheslin (9)	39
Zack Lloyd	40
Jacob (6)	41
Milo Brabbins (9)	42
Cameron Bell (8)	43
Kamal Ahmedi (6)	44
Summer Cox (8)	45
Bella Buckingham (11)	46
Lyla Pardoe (6)	47
Jai Kassim (10)	48
Ella Bourne (9)	49
Angelina Masih (9)	50
Alfie Griffiths (10)	51
Alex Stevenson (7)	52
Alexhia-Louise Pitt (6)	53
Isabella Evans (7)	54
Luke Wang (8)	55
Aariz Wasim (7)	56
Riley Foxall (9)	57
Kaleb Parker Mills (7)	58
Lilly Perkins (10)	59
Archie Hedley (10)	60
Poppy-mai Parkes (9)	61
Skyla Levy (6)	62
Dylan Rio Taylor Edwards (10)	63
Ashton Cole (7)	64
Chloe Peach (10)	65
Bonnie Elwood (7)	66
Georgie Kerfoot (7)	67
Zayn Khan	68
Khizer Shahabaz (7)	69

Gracie Harris-Green (6)	70
Jack Brookes (10)	71
Eleanor Hedley (6)	72
Harley Ellis (9)	73
Esther Dunn (7)	74
Olivah-James Pitt (10)	75
Thomas Bird (8)	76

Hungerford Primary School, Hungerford

Summer Wrzesinski (10)	77
Hannah Green (10)	78
Jessica Cooper (10)	80
Gabrielle King (11)	81
George Collins (11)	82
Zachary Gill (11)	83
Hetti Stone (10)	84
Shayla Daley (11)	85
Logan Gough (10)	86
Poppy Radford (10)	87
Meredith Binns (10)	88
Laurence Hodgkin (10)	89
Harry Rivers (10)	90
Isabel Watton (10)	91
Esmae Fidler (10)	92
Reggie Ponsford (11)	93
Kaia Forte (10)	94
Orla Waters (10)	96
Dylan Cundy (10)	97
Nicole Archer (10)	98
Robyn Sprules (10)	99
Oscar Galbraith (10)	100
Ryan Player (11)	101
Spencer Cukier (10)	102
George Day (11)	103
Mary Smart (10)	104
Felicity Young (10)	105
Lexi Dopson (10)	106
Jessica Edwards (10)	107
Oscar Milne-White (10)	108
Arlyah Kupiec (10)	109
Archie Yates (11)	110
Maria Popescu (10)	111

Josh Pearce (10)	112
Harry Marsh (11)	113
Toby Grainger (10)	114
Kailen Sandell (10)	115
Rhys Berry (10)	116
Max Green (10)	117
Oscar Long (10)	118
George Rhodes (10)	119
Shakira Bulley (11)	120
Charlie Bees (10)	121
Haiden John Harry Pearcey (10)	122
Ethan Proudfoot (10)	123
Leo Roff (11)	124
Zack Thomas (10)	125
Mia Weeks (11)	126
Harley Ward-Little (11)	127

North Primary School, Southall

Omar Farooq Mohammed (10)	128
Mariama Hassan (10)	130
Rafia Rahim Tofa (11)	131
Salina Shamen (10)	132
Simrath Kaur	133
Ayesha Hasan (10)	134
Alina Dehzad (11)	135
Aliyah Kamorudeen (10)	136
Keziah Nimako (10)	137
Monaza Haidari (9)	138

St Francis Catholic Academy, Bedworth

Ianis Mantoiu (8)	139
Travis Dinh (9)	140
Reuben Hundal (9)	141
Max Jones (9)	142
Isabella Pugh (9)	143
Lilith Franklin-Weeks (9)	144
Tanyi Okpu (8)	145
Henry Cowan (9)	146
Olivia Wigmore (8)	147
Lucy Packer (8)	148

St Mary's Catholic Primary School, Loughborough

Serin Durna (10)	149
Nayara Gondar Aboo (11)	150
Mikael Tristanto (11)	153
Victoria Gladiseva (11)	154
Cadee Fung (11)	156

Trinity All Saints CE Primary School, Bingley

Amelia Farooqi (10)	157
Imogen Shackleton (9)	158
Amelia Mason (9)	159
Iris Rubery (10)	160
Aiza Masud (10)	161
Erin Irwin (10)	162
Emily Parker (9)	163

THE POEMS

Dreams With Sienna

D reams are amazing, especially with Sienna,
R eady to go on an adventure with us?
E xcited, we ran around, exploring, and having fun.
A lways best sisters, hooray, let's go.
M ean, mean, mean, what is that? Is that real? I don't think so.
S weets here, sweets there, sweets up, down, and everywhere.

W hat's no? Yes, that's all we say, yes, yes, you can do anything.
I can't believe we're here, it's so pretty, it's so beautiful.
T reats here, wow, they're so good, yum, Sienna, do you like it?
H appily, we sit down, looking at the beautiful sunset.

S o let's never stop, we love sister time.
I t is so pretty at night-time, with all the little stars.
E at sweets, everyone! Eat sweets, everyone!
N othing can stop us now!
N ightmares aren't real, ignore them.
A s morning comes, we wake up, I go into her room, she says, "Livvy, that was the best dream, ever!" and I say, "Let's have the same dream, again, tonight."

Olivia Portman (9)
Hob Green Primary School, Pedmore Field

The Night In The Trenches

R emembering these soldiers, days on days
E xhausted like working all day, making their way through mud
M ind filled with terror, they didn't get their ways
E ndless shivering like they were caved in ice
M y body filled with rage, all they could smell was dead mice
B ody stumbling over; all they could think of was sleep
R eady to fight, UK is war, UK
A lso enable this time please, no more
N ext was to fire the guns
C an only eat horrific cheese and buns
E nd this time, will this ever end?

D on't break your back or you will not bend
A lso, don't forget we never stopped
Y ou and I did the best of all.

Daiton Hill (10)
Hob Green Primary School, Pedmore Field

Sweet Dreams Marnie

S weet dreams are everywhere
W henever you are dreaming
E verywhere you are, you can dream
E veryday you can dream of unicorns
T hen you can dream of rainbows

D ragons maybe you can dream of
R eady or not here come nightmares!
E verywhere you can dream
A nd beware of nightmares.
M arnie don't be scared, it's not real
S ome dreams are bad and some are good

M arnie you are always dreaming
A nd keep dreaming all night
R eady to dream Marnie
N ight night Marnie, sweet dreams
I love you so much, dream good
E verywhere you go there are dreams.

Freya Jones (9)
Hob Green Primary School, Pedmore Field

Fantasy World

When I was walking through the fluffy, soft clouds,
I walked into the sun.
He didn't look too happy,
He wanted to go for a run.
I said to him, "I control the day and night.
We have to wait until the time is right."
He said to me, "Hurry up and make it night then."
"I can't sun, you need to shine above the houses a little bit longer.
The time is not right.
I control the day and night,
I know when the time is right,
The time is not right yet sun."
"Okay, I'll shine a bit longer."
"You don't need to, you can go for a run now, sun.
I control the day and night,
And the time is now right."

Jasmine Taylor (9)
Hob Green Primary School, Pedmore Field

Sugar Rush

As Khalani's mum said, "Good night!"
It gave Khalani such a fright.
Khalani's mum said, "Don't worry, everything's alright,
I'll tuck you into bed and kiss you good night."

So Khalani closed her eyes,
And dreamt of unicorns dashing through the skies.
Then she had a dream of eating loads of ice cream!
All different flavours, stacked high in a tall glass.
Loads of chocolate sauce and cherries... it was class!

So Khalani had a great night's sleep,
Until her alarm clock went *beep! Beep! Beep!*
She opened her eyes and what a surprise!
No unicorns, and no ice cream in sight.

Eva Brazier (11)
Hob Green Primary School, Pedmore Field

Enchanted Forest Dream

Time for bed
To relax my head
I drifted into a sleep
And had an adventurous dream.

I felt a sense of wonder
Towering trees is what I was under
There was a magical feeling
Until I saw a fearsome tiger roaring.

Courageously, he ran past me
I wondered how fast he could be
What caught my eye
Was a rapid cheetah in the tree up high.

There was lots to explore
I wanted to see it all
Like the vibrant colours and unique plants
And the exotic spiders and many ants.

After a journey like never before
I heard a knock on my door
It was time to wake up
From my deep sleep of fun.

Salma Kaid (10)
Hob Green Primary School, Pedmore Field

Bound With Strings

After the show
When all is lost
She climbs into bed
With worries in her head
Praying for a miracle to save her career
As she falls into a comforting slumber
Waking up in a land beyond the stars
In a garden made of strings
A trio of notes come out and go ping
Filling the air with melodies pure and true
Giving her clues on how to cure her blues.
Waking up in a shock
It chimes 12 on the clock
As she dashes downstairs
To a crowd that glares
From a frown to a grin
Laughter and cheering.
The crowd goes wild, smiles for the day
Music can really bring people together
Like bounding them with string.

Zoyal Muqaddas (11)
Hob Green Primary School, Pedmore Field

The Living Nightmare

Bombs dropping, people dying and
no pulse being heard.
Blood splats and dead bodies surround.
People panic and panic.

Bang, bang.

Suddenly, bad news awaits on the doorstep.
Dark clouds come and lightning strikes.
Soldiers run until they can't run anymore,
Guns loading, aim, pointing,
Soldiers crying for peace to rise.
Letters being written in the holy night.

Maybe, if war didn't break out,
If the world had peace,
If the Germans didn't come,
Then my darling princess wouldn't be worrying for her daddy.
My eyes tear up with terror and fright,
Holding my stomach, this could be my final night.

Maddie Bowen (10)
Hob Green Primary School, Pedmore Field

The Crucial Mr Blake

I entered the school as usual,
But didn't know it would turn crucial,
The first lesson began,
With a teacher who was a tall man.

He would make us copy every word from the dictionary,
Luckily for me, I didn't have any stationery.

In the third lesson, I received a call,
And didn't know the happiness would fall,
It was from my dad,
It was in class, so I wasn't glad,
It was as upsetting as a broken heart.

Tears rolled down my eyes,
As Mr Blake looked at me in surprise,
My body did the fake fall,
I woke up and realised it wasn't real at all.

Zaynab Quadoos (11)
Hob Green Primary School, Pedmore Field

Nightmares In The War Ground

I lie in my bed and I fall asleep
A nightmare I keep
I remember the trenches, the way they smell
Mould, rats - is it heaven or hell?
My hands freeze as cold as ice
The Boche aren't very nice
My friend on the floor dead or alive
Dead he is, bye
I am sorry my friend as I miss you
But I am close to dead too
Gas masks, bombs, and trenches too
Oh dear me!
I have lost you
Please come back as I am fighting for life
But I am defeated by fright
I wake up again with my guilt on me
I am afraid I have PTSD.

Lyra Washington (11)
Hob Green Primary School, Pedmore Field

My Dream Place

Slowly floating on a steady and still boat,
I put my hand in the clear blue water,
And to my surprise it wasn't hot or cold.
This was my dream place.
I could tell this was Canada.
Birds chirping,
Leaves blowing,
Suddenly it started snowing.
No better place than here,
I wanted to stay but knew I should go.
I set off for the mountains,
When I got to the top it was dark and cold,
I finally woke after an adventure.
It was a nice dream.
It would have been better in real life...

Leah Taylor (11)
Hob Green Primary School, Pedmore Field

War Nightmare

Through the night,
People march,
Off to fight.
People die,
That's the way,
Of the war.

Through the night,
Soldiers fight,
To win the war.
The wounds of the soldiers,
Being cut bleeding,
Out of their wounded body.

Choking out of the deadly gas,
Through day,
Through night,
Watch each other like a hawk.
Stumbling down,
People die.

Blood splattering,
Drenching the sergeants.

Buddies get lost,
Being shot with a Glock in hand.

Chase Rutherford (11)
Hob Green Primary School, Pedmore Field

Untitled

Ding, ding, ding...
Late for school, a hurried swoosh in my stride.
Gasp...
Excitement rises; the teacher reveals a chocolate factory ride.
Yes!
Whispering at the class's farthest reach, the thrill intensifies.
Twelve minutes later...
We arrive, greeted by a world of chocolate, joy crystallizes.
Indulging in sweet treats and shared delights,
An hour of fun, a memory that ignites.
Home time arrives, wondering if such magic might
Happen again, making each day equally bright.

Yaching Ko (7)
Hob Green Primary School, Pedmore Field

WWII Night

As I lie upon my bed,
The sound of bullets and guns go through my head,
I toss and turn throughout the night,
And think about Dad and Grandad on this night.

I think about how they will fight,
With guns and grenades, with
Bloodshot screams and cries.

I finally go to sleep for the night,
I dream about them all night,
Then I wake up to the war and I'm a nurse helping them all,
Gunshot wounds and all the gore,
I help to heal and make
Better when I kneel to reassure.

Rosie Fletcher (10)
Hob Green Primary School, Pedmore Field

Sweet Dream Alfie

S o when I went to sleep, I had a dream,
W here we went to Candy World.
E at sweets and enjoy.
E at sweets. What?
T ime to eat.

D ig in, everyone. *Dig in everyone.* What!
R eese's
E aster eggs
A cola bottle or two
M altesers

A ero
L iechtensteiner chocolate
F anta
I ce Kool-Aid, nice and blue
E ggnog.

Darcie-Rose Morgan (8)
Hob Green Primary School, Pedmore Field

Nightmares Become Alive

In the night it shall not be bright
Monsters begin to fight all good dreams
Roaming the streets
When it hits 12 they disappear
If you spot a monster they will pick you apart,
Like a piece of corn in your teeth.

Beware if you die in your dream,
You die in real life.
I am not kidding,
They will come for you.
Read carefully and listen to me,
The Backrooms are seriously real.

Good dreams are rare.
Do you care?

Rowan Phipps (11)
Hob Green Primary School, Pedmore Field

Nightmares

N o one was prepared for this
I t was the worst thing in my life
G radually, I started walking
H eavily breathing
T orches hung around the forest lit
M y heart pounding out of my chest
A figure appeared ten steps away from me
R apidly, I started running
E verything started moving around me, trapping me
S taring at the figure, he started chasing me and never stopped.

Tiah Goodwin (10)
Hob Green Primary School, Pedmore Field

The Tale Of The Horse Hero

The horse galloped in the wind
It was heading to the castle
For a young knight
Tall, long-haired
Was going to save all of his already derelict land
A full battalion of cursed ones
They had swords, bows and hammers in their hands
And far in the distance
Glowing lights, shiny, orangey-red fire burst from the dragon's jaws
Seconds later, the army attacked
With a legendary burst of rage
Rushing at the hero.

Ted Price (10)
Hob Green Primary School, Pedmore Field

Nightmares

N othing has ever scared me,
I run for my life! All I see is clowns
G lancing around, I'm tripping over,
H ow did I get here? I hope it's fake.
T hud. A clown appears,
M y worst fear, it's a spooky clown.
A spread of smoke appears around
R unning for my life, it's a clown
E yes glow, it's a clown
S uddenly, I wake up in bed!

Isaac Hammond (8)
Hob Green Primary School, Pedmore Field

Water Park Dream

Boom! I landed at the park.
Woah! Then I saw my best friend Nieve.
I decided that we could go on the zip line.
Swish! And zoom!
We went on the swing and slide
We were having fun, but were starting to get hungry,
So we had some McDonald's, *mmmm!*
The food was delicious.
Then we had a go on the see-saw.
After that we had a picnic,
So we sat by the river to calm down.

Eva-Marie Withers (7)
Hob Green Primary School, Pedmore Field

The Demons That Haunt Me

In the night when the demons haunt me,
I try to sleep. I can't. It may be a dream,
Maybe a nightmare. I look back at it now,
And realise it was a nightmare.
I run away from the demons and try to get shelter,
Sometimes I wonder why they are chasing me,
Now I remember I can't stop running,
I was once a demon... I escaped...
Maybe I should have done it while they were giving kids nightmares...

Olivia Evans (10)
Hob Green Primary School, Pedmore Field

The Man In Black And Blue

Riding in the sky with my friends,
Shocked but wait!
We flew to a lake
Screaming as a monster appeared
We swam and swam.

Flying high over a hill
A man is black and blue
Step by step the man came closer
A friend fell off the hill in a trauma
He laughed an evil laugh.

I woke up by my cat
I thought it was a dream
That scary nightmare kept me awake for days.

Symren Ahmedi (9)
Hob Green Primary School, Pedmore Field

A World Where I'm An Author

A world where I'm an author,
I write lots of books, thousands of books you see,
I write picture books, chapter books, you see,
So go write a book, and you'll be an author like me.
Maybe you could write picture books and storybooks with me,
But we will just have to wait and see,
So come visit me at my book factory,
And we will write lots of books, so just come and see,
Anyone can be an author, just like you and me.

Madison Pritchard (8)
Hob Green Primary School, Pedmore Field

Super Cradley Town DC

Boom!
Three times a week I train for Sunday morning's game,
Up early I get.
Swoosh!
I stand on the field waiting for the whistle to blow,
And the parents to roar, "Here we go."
Hmm... I take my first touch with the ball at my feet,
Anxiously looking up to pass.
My teammates get in the right spot,
Quick pass.
Bangs it in the back of the net.

Max Lewis Shilvock (8)
Hob Green Primary School, Pedmore Field

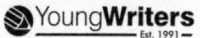

At Hogwarts

Hush!
The wind blew through the branches!

Brring!
The Hogwart's bell went now!

Swoosh!
Harry Potter appeared by me!

Then!
Harry taught me how to do magic.

Now!
That made me really ecstatic.

Bang!
My wand created a spark.

And off I flew on my broom to the park.

Evan Dowler (7)
Hob Green Primary School, Pedmore Field

A Day In WWII

T for troops, getting wrenched along the battlefield.
R for rain, drenching the troops on the battlefield.
E for enemies, soldiers lying dead on the war ground.
N for never-ending war. Will it ever end?
C for cry, a cry for help!
H for horrendous war.
E for enemy gunfire.
S for soldiers, dropping like flies.

Kai Toogood (11)
Hob Green Primary School, Pedmore Field

Untitled

In my dreams every night,
All I see are colours bright.
Magical kingdoms come my way
To Australia every night and day.

Her brown ripped teddy bear
Awaits her sitting on the beach.
Waiting, waiting, waiting, time passes by.

Wondering where her owner has gone,
Morning, noon, night passes,
But not a single star in the sky.

Imogen Lord (11)
Hob Green Primary School, Pedmore Field

Underground Tomb

I had a dream I was underground
With my friends and nothing around
Zombies above us here and there
Who knows if we're ever going to get air
People dead all around us, no music, no sounds
Earthquakes happening all around
Shaking tremors move the ground
Would we survive this horrific scene?
It's worse than being in an awful dream.

Logan Campbell (8) & Musab
Hob Green Primary School, Pedmore Field

Lost On An Island

Slowly floating in the boat
The amazing views seen in the distance
Sunshine shines on me
I woke up to the sky, the shiny bright blue
The feeling of fresh air
I looked around I was on an island
A beautiful island, houses seen in the distance
The post said 'Hawaii, Norway to Hawaii'
Wow, I sank up the feeling.

Jacob Clarke (11)
Hob Green Primary School, Pedmore Field

Under The Water

Under the water,
Sea so warm,
Counting fish,
1, 2, 3, 4.

Everyone hiding,
Watch out, boy!
A fish like this
Ain't a toy.

Big, dark figure,
Like a big fish,
Coming closer,
Watch out, kid!

Eyes open,
Nice warm bed,
Thankfully this dream,
Came to an end.

Mathew Roberts (11)
Hob Green Primary School, Pedmore Field

Darkness

D arkness fills the air,
A damp smell everywhere.
R iding around in a pirate ship,
K indness is no use when you're in an abyss.
N o one here to accompany me,
E ast of sea, I'm gonna be.
S o I'm off to Sydney from the UK,
S ilence comes in the end... Hey!

Hadi Israr (9)
Hob Green Primary School, Pedmore Field

Divide By Zero

The world of Pokémon
In the busy region of Paldea
On the top of its greatest peak
The great crater of Paldea (Area Zero)
There I am catching shark-like Pokémon
Garchomp, flying for my prey
I see a squawkabilly
I hook its wing with my claw
Then biting down with my mighty jaws...
I wake up.

Jenson Brazier (10)
Hob Green Primary School, Pedmore Field

The Dream About Neymar Giving His Shirt To Me

Neymar is giving his shirt to me
And he is clapping and waving at the fans and me.

Neymar is talking to me and he says hi
And the crowd chant to him.

Neymar's hair gel smells like bubblegum
And his toothpaste.

I feel over the moon and excited
Because I got his shirt and he talked to me.

Finley Bell (10)
Hob Green Primary School, Pedmore Field

The Aliens On The Moon

Some giant aliens with petrifying teeth,
Growling monsters staring right at me.
Shooting stars flying all over the place,
With a really fast pace.

The aliens were flying jets,
They were screeching and wailing.
The aliens were growling at me.

Afraid,
Nervous,
Scared,
And terrified.

Jacob Billingham (9)
Hob Green Primary School, Pedmore Field

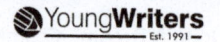

Stuck

I was in a mansion, huge and dark
Down a corridor, a zombie lurked
"Something isn't right," I murmured.
Sweating, I screamed, turned and ran
I could hear their roars behind me,
I ran, and to my surprise this was the only place I could hide,
In the distance I could hear, "Help Me."

Harvey Kerfoot (9)
Hob Green Primary School, Pedmore Field

Nightmares

Nightmares are scary and you
Wouldn't want to have a scary nightmare
You are not scared of blood, are you?
Because nightmares are terrible
Monsters are in your nightmares,
With a teddy on your windowsill, watching you overnight
And spiders crawling over you
Getting lost in a dark, deep forest.

Mia Turner (6)
Hob Green Primary School, Pedmore Field

My Future Dream

In my future dream, I glimpse others in a rhythmic trance,
Fantastic gymnastics unfold, a spectacle to enhance.
Laughter echoes, a symphony of joy in the air,
Rapid breaths, heartbeat racing, excitement rare.
Bitter sweet's aroma whispers tales of success,
In this dream, a journey where dreams coalesce.

Yahei Ko (9)
Hob Green Primary School, Pedmore Field

Football Dreams

D reaming about a footballer is terrific!
R eally good! I literally won a Ballon d'Or.
E uggh! I really want it to be in real life, but you might get a wish.
A lright! Dreams are so annoying sometimes!
M aybe it could happen, legend has it, this could happen in real life.

Liam Cheslin (9)
Hob Green Primary School, Pedmore Field

Dreams

D ragons flying in the shiny, blue sky.
R eading a Harry Potter book to be a wizard.
E pic Harry Potter book to be a good reader.
A wizard came up to me and turned me into a frog,
M y mum takes me to the park.
S ometimes my mum takes me to McDonald's.

Zack Lloyd
Hob Green Primary School, Pedmore Field

Dreams

Everybody loves them and they are magic
Dreams make me happy
Dreams make everything nice
Dreams make things nice
Dreams make me go on my phone
Dreams make me go to my nanny's house
Dreams make me go to my grandad's house
Dreams make me go around the world.

Jacob (6)
Hob Green Primary School, Pedmore Field

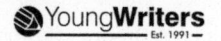

The Dream World

I wake up in a world that I have not explored
I see a lot of wildlife that doesn't exist on Earth
This strange planet has animals such as
The samigobo, facinetev
Parthnef and clabatneath but then
Something starts to chase me
But then I wake up in my own comfy bed.

Milo Brabbins (9)
Hob Green Primary School, Pedmore Field

Football Match

I was at a football pitch with Neymar
And we had a football match
And he scored three goals
And I scored three goals
And I was doing skills
And he was doing skills too
And we did another football match
And I scored eight goals
And he scored eight too.

Cameron Bell (8)
Hob Green Primary School, Pedmore Field

Dreams

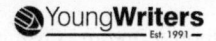

Dreams make me want to go to the beach
Dreams make me go on my phone
Dreams make me go to my grandma's home
Dreams make me go to my dog
Dreams make me go to my bedroom
Dreams make me go to my rabbit
Dreams make me go to the park
Dreams are fabulous.

Kamal Ahmedi (6)
Hob Green Primary School, Pedmore Field

The Glass Maze

I ran around inside a maze,
Something behind me,
A scary clown with a painted face,
His evil laugh rang out loud,
I was by myself so I was terrified,
Everything was made out of glass,
Soon I got lost in the maze,
They almost got me,
I woke up and screamed,
I noticed it was a dream.

Summer Cox (8)
Hob Green Primary School, Pedmore Field

Bad Nightmare

One girl,
One nightmare,
Over 100 ghosts.
I'm losing my head!

I wonder how I ended up here.
Maybe since I ran away from home?
I don't know.
I am sorry.
I really am.
I want to go back.
I want to see my mom...
Boom! Boom!

Bella Buckingham (11)
Hob Green Primary School, Pedmore Field

Nightmares

Nightmares are horrid
Nightmares are spooky
Nightmares are scary
Nightmares have me pulling up the quilt
Nightmares have me falling off a cliff
Nightmares are scary
Nightmares are spooky
Nightmares are horrid
Nightmares are terrifying.

Lyla Pardoe (6)
Hob Green Primary School, Pedmore Field

Racers Senses

F1 car is going super fast
Just like a lightning blast
Tyres screeching, engine roaring
I can't hear any other noises
Smoke rising up to the sky
Clouds which look like cotton candy very, very high
I'm nervous
I'm excited.

Jai Kassim (10)
Hob Green Primary School, Pedmore Field

The Dream Bakery

Delicious cake cooking in the scorching hot oven,
People shouting and screaming for orders.
My tummy growling.
Delicious cake mix transforming into cake and sweet white icing,
Cake icing dribbling down my fingers,
And sprinkles sticking on.

Ella Bourne (9)
Hob Green Primary School, Pedmore Field

Dreams

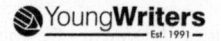

D ragons breathed giant fire.
R ockets and stars shoot up in the night sky.
E veryone likes a magical, beautiful Christmas.
A ngelina wishes to go on a rainbow slide.
M onsters, magic, midnight creeping silently.

Angelina Masih (9)
Hob Green Primary School, Pedmore Field

Dreams

D usty, dazzling new epic Hotwheels cars.
R usty, red and blue, amazing Optimus Prime lorries.
E xcellent epic Villa shirt I got for Christmas.
A mazing rainbow Lego brick.
M y dirtbike, superfast like a Supra!

Alfie Griffiths (10)
Hob Green Primary School, Pedmore Field

Nightmares

Nightmares are scary
Nightmares are terrible
Nightmares make people scream in the night
Nightmares make people get up in the night
Nightmares are dark
Nightmares are black as the dark sky
Nightmares feel like spiders on you.

Alex Stevenson (7)
Hob Green Primary School, Pedmore Field

Dreams

Dreams are amazing
Dreams are wonderful
Dreams happen when you're sleeping, day or night
Dreams are what leave you smiling
Nightmares make you scream
Nightmares leave you scared
Nightmares are waiting for you to sleep.

Alexhia-Louise Pitt (6)
Hob Green Primary School, Pedmore Field

Untitled

Dreams are wonderful.
Dreams are amazing.
Dreams are incredible
Dreams are never bad.
Dreams are magical
You can never beat them.
Dreams are that good
I had a dream of the sea.
Dreams are too good to beat.

Isabella Evans (7)
Hob Green Primary School, Pedmore Field

Dreams

D reaming about being a chef is amazing!
R eading a cook book is interesting!
E ating delicious food is yummy!
A dding the ingredients and a marvellous cake!
M aking marvellous food is amazing!

Luke Wang (8)
Hob Green Primary School, Pedmore Field

Dreams

Dreams are powerful
Dreams make me dash
Dreams make me swim
Dreams make me take my time
Dreams are fabulous
Dreams make heaven
Dreams make me go to school
Dreams are fab
Dreams are just liveable.

Aariz Wasim (7)
Hob Green Primary School, Pedmore Field

Winning A Football Cup

Teammates, football goals
A football and a massive crowd
Chanting fans encouraging me
Delicious food filling the air
Astroturf underneath my feet
Cold air breezing against me
Over the moon, overjoyed.

Riley Foxall (9)
Hob Green Primary School, Pedmore Field

Untitled

D ad is cooking in my dream.
R ed rocket is shooting into space.
E ating dinner.
A healthy superhero.
M om is making pancakes.
S yrup and butter are the best.

Kaleb Parker Mills (7)
Hob Green Primary School, Pedmore Field

The Zombie Story

Huge nasty green zombies
Sharp teeth
Ripped and horrible clothes
Growling
Screaming
Scratching
The smell of garbage
Smelly
Disgusting
I'm scared
I'm terrified.

Lilly Perkins (10)
Hob Green Primary School, Pedmore Field

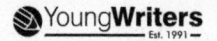

A Footballer's Dream

A ball flying
The referee
Other players
The goalie

The crowd roaring
The crowd jumping
Popcorn falling

Marvellous popcorn

Happy
Excited
Cheerful.

Archie Hedley (10)
Hob Green Primary School, Pedmore Field

A Football Match

A football, a massive crowd of people.
Loud, shouting and cheering.
Tasty popcorn, salty chips and crunchy crisps.
Rough astroturf and the patterned football.
Overjoyed and a bit nervous.

Poppy-mai Parkes (9)
Hob Green Primary School, Pedmore Field

Dreams Are Magic

Dreams are magic.
Some unicorns and horses, and they can talk.
Nightmares are scary and there is shouting.
I saw a dragon blowing a lot of fire.
And I was scared and it made me scream.

Skyla Levy (6)
Hob Green Primary School, Pedmore Field

The Alien On The Moon

Pitch-black void surrounding all around
Terrifying evil alien following everywhere you go
Loud, scary laughing coming from his crater
Hard, white moon rock hurting everyone and everything.

Dylan Rio Taylor Edwards (10)
Hob Green Primary School, Pedmore Field

Untitled

D ragon eating people
R ocket in space
E veryone is playing tag
A superhero's fighting
M agician doing tricks
S ix snakes rolling.

Ashton Cole (7)
Hob Green Primary School, Pedmore Field

The Dream Bakery

Delicious box of confetti cake mix
People telling me lots of orders
Delicious crispy cake mix coming out of the oven
The icing melting on my fingers and
The crunchy sprinkles.

Chloe Peach (10)
Hob Green Primary School, Pedmore Field

Dreams Are Magic

Dreams are magic and wonderful
Beautiful and pretty and lovely and powerful.
And no one knows if you are having a dream,
Only you know who has a clue.
Dreams are marvellous.

Bonnie Elwood (7)
Hob Green Primary School, Pedmore Field

At Night

Nightmares are horrifying things
They are scary too
They make me want to go under the covers
You think monsters are in your wardrobe
You think monsters are under the bed.

Georgie Kerfoot (7)
Hob Green Primary School, Pedmore Field

Untitled

D reams dancing in the woods.
R ocket reaching into the red sky.
E veryone enters quickly.
A ll the people come here every day.
M onster flies into the house.

Zayn Khan
Hob Green Primary School, Pedmore Field

Nightmares

Nightmares are horrible!
Nightmares are spooky!
Nightmares are terrible!
Nightmares make you cry!
Nightmares make you hug your teddy!
Nightmares make you scream!
Ahh!

Khizer Shahabaz (7)
Hob Green Primary School, Pedmore Field

Dreams

Dreams are magical, they make me sleep
Dreams are wonderful
Dreams are incredible
Dreams are my favourite
Dreams are amazing
Dreams make me fly in the sky.

Gracie Harris-Green (6)
Hob Green Primary School, Pedmore Field

Football Dream

D ancing football players.
R onaldo played football.
E veryone cheered loudly like a lion.
A mazing football players.
M essi won the World Cup.

Jack Brookes (10)
Hob Green Primary School, Pedmore Field

Dreams

Dreams take you to the beach
Dreams are amazing
Dreams are magical
Dreams don't exist
Dreams have spaceships
Dreams are marvellous.

Eleanor Hedley (6)
Hob Green Primary School, Pedmore Field

Untitled

D rake comes on stage
R eady to perform
E veryone screams
A fter the show
M oney was thrown.

Harley Ellis (9)
Hob Green Primary School, Pedmore Field

Dreams

Dreams make me want to sleep through the whole entire world.
Dreams are magic.
Dreams make me live in a wonderful fun world.

Esther Dunn (7)
Hob Green Primary School, Pedmore Field

Bubbles

I hope to be an engineer.
I wish to have no fear.
I have a teddy bear.
I give it lots of care. Yeah!

Olivah-James Pitt (10)
Hob Green Primary School, Pedmore Field

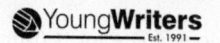

The Amazing Dream

In my dreams every night,
Lamborghinis and Fords.
I am on a highway,
But everyone crashes.

Thomas Bird (8)
Hob Green Primary School, Pedmore Field

My Dream World

M y dream world opened to me as I was drowned in sleep,
Y ou're here like a ray of light, a crowd appeared,
D ing, a cream toffee light slid down just for me,
R ivers of orange juice sparkled in the golden syrup sunlight,
E xcitedly I danced into the light, dark chocolate trees spun around me making me feel dizzy,
A mazing ambers escorted me through the Haribo halls,
M arshmallow puddings skipped and giggled all around,
W orlds are strange sometimes, but it was worth it for now,
O reos took me downstairs. *Bang!* A feast lay before me,
R ations at home are horrible but this is royalty,
L ush pizza melted in my mouth, the hot chocolate was superb,
D read filled my body, I had woken and I would have to face the day.

Summer Wrzesinski (10)
Hungerford Primary School, Hungerford

Nightmares

Nightmares will come,
They always do,
Coming to feast on you!

Millions of eerie eyes blinking rapidly,
Millions of careful cats slinking silently,
Millions of creepy clowns winking weirdly.

Nightmares creep and crawl into your head,
To fill you up, right up with dread,
Then *pop!* They're there in your mind,
And they're not there to be kind.

Hyenas cackling like wicked witches,
Snakes smile like a clown giggling,
Spiders snigger while scattering in the shadows.

Towers of obsidian and gold,
With bricks of slate so bold,
They will use you as bait,
And then it is just too late!

Bam! You're awake and it was just a big mistake.
Sigh! You're lying in bed with no thoughts in your head.

What a night! What a roller coaster of emotions! What a nightmare!

Hannah Green (10)
Hungerford Primary School, Hungerford

My Revolting Teacher

My revolting teacher who is revolting as could be
Gave me lots of homework and made me read
Now I sit at home as bored as a bee with no honey.

My revolting teacher who is revolting as could be
Made me prance and dance while dressed up as a little green pea.

My revolting teacher who is revolting as could be
Made me summersault on top of a TV!
I was spinning end on end
When will this crazy day end?

My revolting teacher who is revolting as could be
Made me act like a frog and go in a bog
Now I'm looking kind of funny while my teacher is
Making money out of my misery.

My revolting teacher who is revolting as could be
Made me run round and round a tree
Why? I ask
Why do you do this to me?
But then I wake up and remember it's just a dream.

Jessica Cooper (10)
Hungerford Primary School, Hungerford

My Happy Place

Snow-covered mountains, that's all I see.
The winking moon looking at me.
I'm in my forest, at least, I think,
Trying to awake myself, as I blink.

I see jars upon jars full of colour and wonder.
Boom! Bang! Crash! Was that thunder?
I hear whales cooing now, I'm sure.
I feel happier. Should I dream more?

Now, I think this is where I belong,
Stalked by curious creatures so long,
I feel unusual. What's next? I say,
I feel different in a wonderful way.

Here, I can do anything, lie down and dream.
Would the whispering trees wonder where I've been?
How did I get here? Where do I belong?
All of this reminds me of a song.

I hum a song till I fall asleep.
Like a secretive chamber, I didn't know
Dreams could wander so deep.

Gabrielle King (11)
Hungerford Primary School, Hungerford

The Magic Potion

Shhh!
My dad told me never to go here
Shhh!
Maybe it's his biggest fear?
Shhh!
Anyway, I sneaked into the full-to-the-brim, mysterious room
Shhh!
I opened my eyes, and then...
Badaboom!

There was a potion glowing green
My dad's face screwed up angry and mean...

I took the potion and gave it a blow
Then the green acid began to flow
I drank it and something felt weird,
Then my dad had vanished... disappeared!
The potion was gleaming, my dad was leaving, was I dreaming?

I woke up and got out my bed
But an emerald-green glow came out of my head
I looked in the mirror, it was the same potion gleaming.
How is that possible? Am I still dreaming?

George Collins (11)
Hungerford Primary School, Hungerford

Colour Catastrophe

Bang! A flash of colour
Everyone's here and they want to discover
Rainbows everywhere, no white or black

Him and I, a world of adventure
Just come with me and we can do it together
Towns and cities go by but it's only us... Him and I
Soaring through the air, together we fly

Like a paint palette, the world looks great
Nothing bland, nothing faint
From up here, the world's a dream
No fear, just calm and serene

Whoosh, swoosh... I fall through the sky
Dancing, twirling and swirling colours pass me by
Bang! A flash of colour
I fall to my feet
Everyone's back and they long to discover.

Zachary Gill (11)
Hungerford Primary School, Hungerford

Imaginary Room

I had a dream, or was it a nightmare?
I was in a room,
My vision was blurred,
I could barely see.
Doors were slamming like bombs exploding in the sky.
Screeching from upstairs, ringing in my ear.
A bright light shone in the night,
A person was hiding behind the door,
Red eerie eyes stared at me.
Another 100 glowing eyes rose from the darkness,
I was getting dizzy.
I was sure I was going insane...
Crunch! Leaves crunching outside the window distracted me,
I made it out! Outside, glowing gorgeously was a mysterious book.
A snowdrop drooping,
A blossom blooming,
The wind zooming.
Leaves on the trees whistling.
Was it over?

Hetti Stone (10)
Hungerford Primary School, Hungerford

The Mysterious Treehouse In A Creepy Garden!

"Ssh! It's a secret."
"Ssh!" I said
That's what Mum always told us...

Our mysterious new abode
With its creepy treehouse
In the spooky, scary secret garden
"Never go in," demanded Mum
Why is there a secret?

Should we go in or should we not?
It was like the treehouse was...
Summoning, telling us to come over.
"Mum's asleep, let's go in."
Quiet as a mouse we entered...

A mythical, mysterious portal twirling
Rainbows and dazzling lights lured us in.
Whoosh! Boing! Pop! Time flew,
Land of Sweets!
Yum!
Where next?

Shayla Daley (11)
Hungerford Primary School, Hungerford

Hanging Off The Edge

The edge of metal clutching
Hard, falling low, dying slower,
After all, it was me hanging to life, it's the life or death
Moments when you think but the crunch of
The bar was the end of the line.

All the movies, all the scenes,
All the pictures, all the dreams,
Hanging off the life of your own,
And as pure as snow my white hands
Went straight red forgetting about life.

Dreaming more, dreaming what, what would happen?
Will you fall? All hope lost, gone
From this world, falling slowly, thudding
The ground, waking up slow,
Finally awake, from this dream or from death alone.

Logan Gough (10)
Hungerford Primary School, Hungerford

The Nightmare School

In my dream I visited an alien world
And I picked up a travel guide.

Here are the top ten places to go:

The crystal waterfall that is as clear as the light blue sky
The gingerbread house that is crunchy and delicious
The ocean sea as bright as the sun
The pirate ship full of gold
The dancing snowman on the highest mountain
A creepy, crawly wood of adventures
Cotton candy volcano filled with various types of sweets
Amazing strawberry and blueberry milkshake shack
Clouds as fluffy as marshmallows in the sky
You cannot miss this one, the cave of Stone-Age man.

Poppy Radford (10)
Hungerford Primary School, Hungerford

Off To Dreamland

Psst! Over here! Let's go to Dreamland!
We're drifting off and dreaming,
So will you please stop screaming.

A spider starts to make his speech,
"You see that platform up above,
That platform is the one we'll reach,
Full of dancing meadows and lots of fun,
Let's not go to the area with no sun."

Off we flew and flew and flew,
We reached the island,
Yahoo!

Suddenly we hear a booming voice,
It shouts as loud as a fog horn,
We have no choice!

Out of Dreamland we come,
Oh no! It's our teacher!
Run!

Meredith Binns (10)
Hungerford Primary School, Hungerford

This Is Not A Dream

This is not a dream
However strange and horrible it seems
Your smile will instantly turn upside down and into a frown
Welcome to my room, the lights are off
The house is quiet but my mother never heard me
For my brother had a cough
I saw my toy dog as white as snow
I thought it was still but now I don't know
Suddenly the toy dog was no longer on the bed
And was chasing me instead
With a great big *bang!* I ran into the door
I pushed it too and then ran some more
I then went back into my room, where was the dog?
He was on the bed where it all started
What a day! I thought then the dog gave me a nod.

Laurence Hodgkin (10)
Hungerford Primary School, Hungerford

Last Night I Had A Dream

I was sitting in my emerald garden
Wishing for a tree
Suddenly my face filled with glee
I looked around
And out of the ground
There appeared a tree!

I was looking up in awe
When I saw
A mythical beast rustling through the leaves
As it flew into the sky like a rocket lifting off
It landed on the loft
The wind whistled
And the tree swayed
A dragon landed on the floor
I looked around and saw more.

Suddenly, I was surrounded
By creatures, I was looking at their fantastic
Features when I awoke
Now every night I hope.

Harry Rivers (10)
Hungerford Primary School, Hungerford

The Man In My Wardrobe

The man in my wardrobe is as fast as lightning,
He's gone in a flash, it's rather frightening,
He comes at night, never to be seen,
Sometimes I can feel him, lurking in my dreams.
The man in the wardrobe can sometimes move,
Once I caught him in the glove,
Most every night, after that I heard a creaky creak
Other than that he does not make a peep.
He's as quiet as a mouse,
Except once, he came out with a big crash and bang,
And he screamed out ouch
I've never seen him before
If you didn't clearly would not be a chore
But for now, sleep tight
Don't let the man in the wardrobe bite.

Isabel Watton (10)
Hungerford Primary School, Hungerford

The Day With The Ghost

"Hush don't go in,"
I said, "No."
Hush. End of discussion.

A giant, creepy haunted house.
"Don't go in," Mother always says
Hush, end of discussion.

The house kept calling
"Come in, come in."
Whoosh! A gust of wind lured us in
Creak! The door opened wide, and we
Stepped in.

Panic. My heart was racing
As a ghost slipped out of the shadows
Boom. The floor collapsed,
A purple portal appeared
And drew us into a
World of imaginations.

Esmae Fidler (10)
Hungerford Primary School, Hungerford

Whilst I Sleep

Whilst I sleep
I sit there and lay
I sit there and wonder
What's going to happen today?

Now I am writing a book with Charles Dickens,
Then leading a flock of white puffy chickens.

I am now becoming a superhero,
Even though my strength is zero.

Whilst flying through the air with a swish and a swoosh,
I find a hungry grizzly bear in a bush.

It is fierce, strong but so hazy,
From skipping down the road picking daisies.

Now I turn to see I am in an abyss,
Where there is no hope, no freedom, no bliss.

Reggie Ponsford (11)
Hungerford Primary School, Hungerford

At The Zoo

Swing, stomp
I was free.
I was out.
Venturing into the grass.
Was I free at last?

The sun set like a lamp switched off.
And my nose was filled with the foul smell,
Of cow pats,
Oh, what a dread.
Still, I continued to follow my path.
Was I free at last?

There it was, freshly cut grass.
Oh, how it blocked my throat.
Cough, splatter.
There was a boat.

I set sail on the back of the boat.
Stars danced.
Mars pranced.
There I was at the end of the line.
To redeem all of the lost time.

There were foxes there, badgers too,
Oh, how I love it at the zoo.

Kaia Forte (10)
Hungerford Primary School, Hungerford

Looking Out My Window One Night

Looking out my window, one night,
I heard a noise, a crash, a bang!
Then all went quiet like there was nothing there.
But I knew there was, I swear.
There was a shadow, like an inky black sky.
The only thing that I could see was the diamond-dazzling eyes.
But I thought it could all be lies.

I climbed out my window one night to a fiery dragon light.
We rode through the night,
Having a glimpse of each and every sight.
Never getting tired,
Never getting bored,
But I was back in my bed safe and sound.
The dragon wasn't even around.
Maybe a dream?
Maybe not?
Looking out my window one night.

Orla Waters (10)
Hungerford Primary School, Hungerford

Imagination

When I close my eyes I can see
A world of pure imagination
While I'm there I can see
My wildest dreams and creations

As I fly through the sky
I see into my imagination
Embracing the strange and marvellous
Sights that are a sensation

The colours splatter everywhere
Like a toddler painting on a canvas
The sun beams down on me
With a warm smile on its face

Crazy, creepy clowns chase me
Through the night, their eyes glowing bright
Suddenly, I fly awake in bed
And realise it was all in my head.

Dylan Cundy (10)
Hungerford Primary School, Hungerford

Nightmares

N ightmares, nightmares,
I dreamt about getting lost.
G reat? I think not!
H eaded toward the middle of nowhere, the grass tickles my feet.
T his isn't funny! It's as quiet as a mouse.
M ummy? Where are you? The sea is roaring!
A nd there is no civilisation, buildings fewer.
R ivers flowing, as dirty as the sewers,
E ast, west, south, north, I don't know where I am. *Thud!* What's that? I'm full of dread.
S tars come alive again. I'm at last in my bed!

Nicole Archer (10)
Hungerford Primary School, Hungerford

I Had A Nightmare

N ightmares, they ruin wonderful dreams.
I nside them, no one knows what they mean.
G igantic giants *thud!* Squishy towns under their feet.
H ungry hobgoblins stealing all sorts of
T hings like beets.
M alicious men watching me like a hawk all day.
A ngry apes yelling in my ear, "Get out of our forest, you don't belong here!"
R aging rhino, charging near.
E lectric eels slithering like snakes into your bed.
S pooky spiders dangling like stars over your leg.

Robyn Sprules (10)
Hungerford Primary School, Hungerford

Getting Ever Taller

Lots of people in the crowd,
Just make me really proud.
I'm right there on the pitch,
But is it just a glitch?
I seem to be growing taller,
And I'm definitely not getting smaller,
I guess I'm just a footballer,
Getting ever taller.
Is it just a dream?
I guess I'm on the pitch with my team.
The colour I'm wearing is blue,
And I'm wearing the number two.
I realise I'm growing taller,
And I'm definitely not getting smaller,
I guess I'm just a footballer,
Getting ever taller.

Oscar Galbraith (10)
Hungerford Primary School, Hungerford

Nightmares

N ightmares, I know they're not the greatest.
I know they maybe send scary shivers down your spine.
G o there and see creatures so deadly
H urry, they're going to kill you.
T here are many different; you have been here many days.
M ore creatures are coming, they shall find you, don't stop.
A fter dark they will not stop, no matter what.
R un. They're right behind you, they are like cheetahs running after their prey.
E ven though they have got you, *bang*.
S top sleeping, wake up!

Ryan Player (11)
Hungerford Primary School, Hungerford

Nightmares

N ightmares, nightmares, as quick as can be,
I will cry when they come,
G reen goblins stealing everyone,
H ow did they get here, how am I here?
T hud, something falls, what is it now?
M y worst fear is crawling around,
A black, hairy ball, why, why, why?
R unning, sprinting, a spider, it's small,
E erie spiders, crawling on me, jumping, speeding, as fast as can be,
S uddenly, you're back at home, don't be afraid, you're not alone.

Spencer Cukier (10)
Hungerford Primary School, Hungerford

Nightmare

N ightmares come and go, they always will
I took a deep breath. *Thud!* The basement door slammed shut
G eared up, I was ready to fight
H ideous as hyenas ready to strike
T here they were, giving me a fright
M y senses kicked in and I ran as fast as I possibly could
A s soon as I glanced back, I was shocked to see them with my eyes
R unning like Usain Bolt, they started to chase
E asily, they caught up; I closed my eyes, and there was Mum.

George Day (11)
Hungerford Primary School, Hungerford

I Dreamt Of...

I dreamt of...
Sparkling rivers, dancing fairies,
Dazzling unicorns, gleaming spirits.

I dreamt of...
Shining stars, twinkling moons,
Whirling galaxies, prancing planets

I dreamt of...
Dragons and rainbows and tropical birds
But then all of a sudden

I dreamt of...
Eerie mist, sinister ruby-red eyes,
Murky water, lapping at my feet, *splash, splash, splash*

Out of the shadows, a looming shape,
The baron of blood, the Nightmare King...

I dreamt of...
A beautiful nightmare.

Mary Smart (10)
Hungerford Primary School, Hungerford

Fireworks

F ireworks prancing, dancing with the stars
I watch the black sky painted with colours
R ound me people watching mesmerised
E nchanting flashes, booms and crashes
W ow, look, that one's spinning like a Ferris wheel
O oh, that one's whooshing
R uby red, emerald green, the most perfect colours I've ever seen
K een to watch them all night long
S leeping peacefully in my bed, has this all happened in my head?

Felicity Young (10)
Hungerford Primary School, Hungerford

The Galaxy Wolf

The Galaxy Wolf comes once a year,
The footsteps ringing through the ear.
Past the moon, past the stars,
The secret whispers that come from Mars,
The dancing daisies from afar swirl all around in the dark.

The majestic patterns imprint on the clouds,
The looming fireflies twirling all around,
The fresh roars of the rain,
The singing doves echoing in my brain.

The Galaxy Wolf came this night of the year,
Was it just a dream?
I swear it was real.

Lexi Dopson (10)
Hungerford Primary School, Hungerford

He's Here

He's there creeping through the forgotten shadows
The whispering wind follows him
He does not walk, he glides with the shadows,
The whispering wind follows him
In my old-fashioned room blood trails him red as fire
The whispering wind follows him

His eyes are cold
He is a ghost
Creak
His teeth are daggers
He is a ghost
A glint of silver above my bed
I wake
The whispering wind comes from the shadows
He's here.

Jessica Edwards (10)
Hungerford Primary School, Hungerford

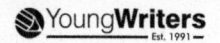

This Is Not Spain

I'm in a plane, I'm excited to go to Spain!
Apart from the storm, that takes my excitement away!

Suddenly a bang, I cover my ears!
I can't see anything, it's increased my fears!

I open my eyes...

It's like nothing happened,
Perhaps I just imagined?

Everyone around me, still as a rock.
I hear ticking, but there is no clock.

People walk towards, what is going on?
Am I in Spain, what is going on?

Oscar Milne-White (10)
Hungerford Primary School, Hungerford

My Dream

In my dream I saw
A sunflower dancing underneath the drooping sun.

In my dream I saw
A delicious cheesy moon dripping onto Earth.

In my dream I heard
The clouds crying, birds chirping and wind swirling.

In my dream I heard
The roaring of a monster coming closer and closer.

In my dream I saw
A mystical waterfall shimmering like a fresh diamond.

In my dream I heard
The beckoning call of my mum waking me up.

Arlyah Kupiec (10)
Hungerford Primary School, Hungerford

The Big Red

In my dream,
I was in a spaceship,
I was amazed.

In my dream I heard,
The sound of engines going by,
They went roar in the space sky.

In my dream I saw,
An alien spaceship on Mars,
It started to fly to the stars.

In my dream I heard,
I heard the laughing of the green man.
He said, "My name is Dan."

In my dream I saw,
Dan grinning at us with his scary face,
He started to give chase.

Archie Yates (11)
Hungerford Primary School, Hungerford

It Was Just A Dream, Or Was It?

It was just a dream, or was it?
Half asleep, half awake
Oh, for goodness sake
Standing up, stretching wide
I look in the mirror in my eyes...

In the corner of my eye, out the window outside
I see the stars dancing through
And next to it, was me and you
You swoop me up in the sky to a planet where I'll fly

I'm back in bed with one eye open
Silent sounds not even a chime

It was just a dream, or was it?

Maria Popescu (10)
Hungerford Primary School, Hungerford

Car Ride

C ome on," they said, "we need to get snacks,"
A s quick as a flash to get back on the tracks
R ight at that moment, the car started to go with no one in control

R acing down like a pro, shouting, *pop, bang!*
I t just kept on going and flowing
D riving and riding, I wondered why
E verything suddenly stopped; I realised they didn't fill the petrol up.

Josh Pearce (10)
Hungerford Primary School, Hungerford

The Nightmare

Relentless, torturous, months on end,
I twist and turn in the night, I'm scared.
He screams and cackles,
I curl up in a ball and cry and weep.

The night has come,
Nightmare is here.

I run and run till I can't no more,
Nightmare is here.
The water soaks up in my nightgown
Once again I curl up in a ball and weep.

Nightmare is here,
His greasy hair dances in the windy gust.
Nightmare is here,
He haunts me
Tears pour out
I cry and scream.

Harry Marsh (11)
Hungerford Primary School, Hungerford

The Magic Book

In my dream, I opened a book
A magic mist danced and pranced in the air
It teleported me, without a care
A smooth, metallic castle stood, in the air so tall and fair
The moonlight shone... so strong upon
The enchanted wood where my castle stood
It teleported me, without a care
Back to the start, as quick as a dart
The magic mist closed the book
There I stood, in the wood
Book in hand
Where I stand
In my dream, I opened a book.

Toby Grainger (10)
Hungerford Primary School, Hungerford

My Nightmare

In my nightmare, I saw
A dark, empty road, far away from civilisation

In my nightmare, I heard
Footsteps that filled the vicinity, echoing in the darkness

In my nightmare I saw
A dark, dishevelled man, standing, staring my soul down

In my nightmare, I felt
An ominous feeling I've never felt before; I was frozen still

In my nightmare
He was gone...

Kailen Sandell (10)
Hungerford Primary School, Hungerford

Dreams And Nightmares

Some dreams are good,
Some dreams are bad,
Some dreams you wish you never had,
Some, like nightmares, they ruin your night,
And they give you quite a fright,
Nightmares have booms, bangs and lots of screams!
And in some dreams, people are mean,
Some dreams, things go wrong,
But in some, you get strong,
But as soon as you wake up
You will forget it all if you have good luck.

Rhys Berry (10)
Hungerford Primary School, Hungerford

Helping Someone And Getting A Fee, A Trillion Pounds!

Crash!
Hit by a car.
I tried to help out.
Crowds, chaos and confusion,
But they were knocked out.
Before he left me,
His smile faded away, like waves at sea.
He gave me a fee,
A trillion pounds! I am dynamite!
I spent it all,
Fame and fall.
The engine roared.
Hit by a car, he tried to help out,
I left him a fee.

Max Green (10)
Hungerford Primary School, Hungerford

Once Upon A Dream

In my dream, I am sat
on the swaying grass
as it tickles my feet.

In my dreams, I can see the
neo-purple galaxy with diamond-like
stars in the background of
Mystical planets.

In my dream, I see a star that is
glowing gold, so I get my trusty
rod and pull it out of the sky.

In my dream, anything is possible.

Oscar Long (10)
Hungerford Primary School, Hungerford

Magical World

In my dream, I saw,
Orange orangutans jumping in and out of the sea like dolphins.

In my dream, I saw
Big fluffy unicorns dancing on rainbows.

In my dream, I saw
Animals at work, humans swimming and climbing.

In my most fantastic dream, I saw
James Bond doing ballet with an elephant.

George Rhodes (10)
Hungerford Primary School, Hungerford

I Had A Dream

I had a dream,
It was a serious scheme.
In it, was a queen with a delicious dream.

I had a dream,
I was eating bouncing beans.
With the queen with delicious dreams.

I had a dream,
The queen who was eating beans and bouncing with delicious dreams,
Farted with a delicious scream!

Shakira Bulley (11)
Hungerford Primary School, Hungerford

Panda

Pandas dance and prance,
They travel to faraway places like France,
Pandas play netball,
They tumble and fall,
Pandas eat pasta,
They sing reggae rasta,
Pandas whisper and giggle,
They like to wiggle,
Pandas make swiss roll,
They always score the winning goal,
Pandas make me happy and free,
Come with me and you will see.

Charlie Bees (10)
Hungerford Primary School, Hungerford

The Battered Bunker

In my dream, I saw
A bold, battered and beaten bunker
The bunker has an indoor farm
There were cameras everywhere.

In the bunker there were
British soldiers
They were hiding from the German troops
The bunker was in Britain
In the bunker, there was a slipping, splashy pool.

Haiden John Harry Pearcey (10)
Hungerford Primary School, Hungerford

Concert Of The Ages

Murmurs fill the air.
Cheers ring out from the crowd.
I've come a long way,
More than a mile away.
The Paris stage stares back at me.
Chaotic claps echo,
Thud, thud, thud.
I had a dream in Paris,
The yelling of the microphone still echoes in my head.
I wake up, it's all gone,
Still lying in my bed.

Ethan Proudfoot (10)
Hungerford Primary School, Hungerford

I'm Lost

Suddenly I trip
I'm falling through the darkness, which is swallowing me
It makes me think I am lost

Strangers swirling past me, they look like ghostly ghosts
Butterflies are in my tummy
I'm lost!

I suddenly wake up In my bed
All the butterflies disappear
I am now safe at home
In my bed.

Leo Roff (11)
Hungerford Primary School, Hungerford

My Dream: Rugby

R ugby is an amazing game, it's a class above
U nder the lights, they can shout your name and show you love
G etting muddy is part of the job
B y the way, football's a mob
Y ou're my game, rugby, I love.

Zack Thomas (10)
Hungerford Primary School, Hungerford

The Flying Broomsticks

In my dream I saw
Wicked, wiry and withered witches
Their broomsticks flew like motorbikes

In my dream, I heard
An evil eagle making loud noises

In my dream, I saw
A slippery, slimy snake, slithering through the sand.

Mia Weeks (11)
Hungerford Primary School, Hungerford

It Was A Dream?

I can see flashing, crashing,
Fireworks springing and jumping at the sky.
Red, blue, pink, green,
Booming, zooming, whooshing.
Small, medium, colossal,
Fantastic fireworks fill the night sky.
Just me absorbing the view,
In my dream, fireworks and me.

Harley Ward-Little (11)
Hungerford Primary School, Hungerford

I Had A Dream Last Night

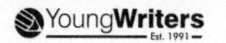

I had a dream last night,
I'm a superhero, mighty and bright.
Wearing a magical cape, I fly
Up high in the vast blue sky.

Above a city filled with light and beam,
Children full of hope and gleam.
They look at me, all happy and cheery,
Waving their hands, playing a symphony.

A villainous laughter echoes through the air.
Oh! What is that? I stare...

A villain, evil and malevolent,
Enter the city so benevolent.
With a wicked smile, flying over Dover,
He says, "This city will be mine!"
Taking over...

I see his wicked minions,
Bringing dark clouds in gazillions.

Clouds of misery surrounding the city,
Global warming and poverty.

Kindness gone, bringing grief,
Rising costs, no relief.

Infuriated and enraged,
I use my super laser all flared.

The villain and his minions are hit,
Falling face down over grit.

Dusk clouds retreat,
Fresh breeze to breathe.

Wind turbines twirl,
What a magical swirl!

Smiles so bright,
Rainbow delight.

Kindness takes over grief;
What a relief!

With high hopes, I take flight.
As the city bathes in eco-light.
Free from hunger, free from fight,
I had a dream last night.

Omar Farooq Mohammed (10)
North Primary School, Southall

The White Coat

I listen to the heartbeats of a dream,
The steady rhythm of a noble goal,
To heal the wounds and ease the pain,
To mend the body and the soul,

I follow the heartbeat of a dream,
Through years of study and sacrifice,
To learn the art and science of medicine,
To gain the skill and pay the price,

I share the heartbeat of a dream,
With those who walk the same path as me,
To support each other and collaborate,
To grow together and make history,

I feel the heartbeat of a dream,
With every patient that I will meet,
To connect with them and empathise,
To treat them with respect and dignity.

I live the heartbeat of a dream,
With passion, compassion and curiosity,
To become a doctor and save lives,
To fulfil my dream and destiny.

Mariama Hassan (10)
North Primary School, Southall

Future Plans

In the future, I want to make the world a better place.
I'll try to make that work if I can.
I can start that by putting a smile on someone's face.

In the future, I want to make a difference in the world,
Helping the poor as much as I can.
Maybe even put racism to an end,
Or help out a friend.

In the future, I want to be a hero.
I stare out my window every day and think,
Can I fly?
I might as well try!
Or maybe not... I might die.

In the future, I want to face my fear,
Oh how much I hate spiders!
Creepy-crawlies all around,
Eight legs and maybe thousands of eyes.
Who knows what they can do to you...

Rafia Rahim Tofa (11)
North Primary School, Southall

Getting Lost

Good morning, I say to myself,
But this was not morning and I did not know where I was.

Eventually, I realised no one was with me, which made me even more scared as I was walking down the abandoned village.

Trembling with fear, I heard something rustle through the bushes.

Terrified of what I heard, I ran as quickly as I could.

Immediately, I ran and came across a bakery and rushed inside.

Not knowing, I'd leave this place alive. I thought of a solution that could help me.

Good thing I had my cell phone on me, but when I called someone, I realised I had no signal.

Lost and lonely, I still look for a place to stay.

Salina Shamen (10)
North Primary School, Southall

Dreaming Superhero

As I was soaring across the sky,
I saw people as small as ants,
When I touched the brown, dry petal,
It sprang back to life,
Teleporting at the speed of light
To give the bad guys a fright.
Holding back an avalanche as light as a feather,
I can use my super strength even in cold weather.
I can read a villain's mind,
So when they come I will give them a surprise.
I hope you enjoy this dream,
But now it is time for me to wake up.

Simrath Kaur
North Primary School, Southall

Dreamy Dreams

Knights and bikes
Children with kites
Genies and wishes
Cars with crashes
Humans with rights
Bullies with fights
Unicorns and fairies
Dinosaurs with berries
Mermaids with tales
Prisoners in jail
Royals demanding
Servants obeying
Birds chirping
Frogs leaping
Horses being ridden
Lions chasing people
Next, there's a sequel.

Ayesha Hasan (10)
North Primary School, Southall

Boom!

Boom! Boom! Boom!
Children play peacefully, until
Parents call kids inside.
Babies get taken to the countryside.

"Mum, what's that sound?"
Families go to bunkers.
While kids wait in hunger.

Sirens stop.
Mothers wait in silence.
People leave bunkers,
And people's hunger fades away.

Kids get to play,
As mothers get to say,
"I love you."

Alina Dehzad (11)
North Primary School, Southall

Moonlit Sky

The moonlit sky,
Every night, I come by.
The moon so bright,
Just in the magical night.

The beautiful stars,
Made with Mars.
The moon is covered in mist,
As I hold my wrist.

The magic air is tingling,
Protected by eaglings.
Flying across the night air,
Plucking the pear.

Aliyah Kamorudeen (10)
North Primary School, Southall

Dreams

Dreams are scary
Dreams can make you weary

Dreams are fun
They can make you reach for the sun

Dreams are sad
Some can make you mad

Dreams feel you
They can even heal you

Dreams open your imagination
Dreams inspire your creation

Dreams are prettier than they seem...

Keziah Nimako (10)
North Primary School, Southall

Flying High

Flying high in the sky,
So high above I can't even lie.
Birds fly by as I fly,
Dreams aren't true until you try.
I'm so high I can't even spy,
Hope I'm not allergic to feathers
Because this is a bad sign,
Heaven must be near.
Goodbye, I hope you don't mind.

Monaza Haidari (9)
North Primary School, Southall

Hand In Hand

A dream about an idol,
Me and a lot of people share,
A dream about me,
For which I am prepared.

A dream that seems so real,
Although it isn't normal,
My hero appears in sight,
He's coming from the paranormal.

He's taller than I imagined,
But brings the same light,
And a silence falls as Ronaldo appears in sight.

For me, he's more than just a name,
He's a hero in a beautiful game,
Through highs and lows, I stand by his side,
A passion which I carry with pride.

The morning comes and dreams go away,
But the memory is like a sunny day,
And it will always remain in my heart,
I met my idol, hand in hand.

Ianis Mantoiu (8)
St Francis Catholic Academy, Bedworth

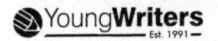

Teacher

In the hallowed halls of knowledge's embrace,
A beacon of guiding grace,
Stands a teacher steadfast and true,
With lessons to impart and dreams to pursue.

With knowledge and grace they sculpt and mould,
Helping us navigate worlds yet untold.
They paint on the canvas of young hearts,
Leaving impressions that never depart.

Their words are like melodies, sweet and clear.
Soft whispers of guidance, erasing the fear.
In classrooms adorned with stories of old,
Their passion for learning a tale to be told.

Through laughter and passion they pave the way
For minds to blossom for the stars
Fuelling the flame that burns from afar.

Travis Dinh (9)
St Francis Catholic Academy, Bedworth

Candyland Cottage

Candyland Cottage is a place in my dreams,
When the clock struck ten I heard the sound of feet,
I opened my eyes, excited, who will I meet?

Stood in front of me was a crazy man with a white long beard,
He showed me my emotions, what made me happy, sad and the things I feared,
We walked through the valley filled with mystical creatures and beast,
He made me walk quickly because soon we will feast,
I was confused at what he meant but followed a sandy path,
Amazingly at the end is a cottage made of candy,
We ate so much candy and had so much fun,
But the sound of the alarm meant the dream was done.

Reuben Hundal (9)
St Francis Catholic Academy, Bedworth

Sweet Dreams

Once upon a dream,
There was a magical scene,
Candyfloss clouds,
Gently flew above the gathering crowds,
Breathtaking sugar dragons,
Shot across the sugar apple-filled wagons.

For this sweet land,
For this special plan,
Squish your toes in the sugar sand,
This is a place for friends,
Where the fun never ends.

The sugar fairies and sweet humbugs,
They cast spells and drink drugs,
We managed to catch them in mugs,
But the sweets begin to come alive,
Five by five,
Here comes the war,
Against the sweets below...

Max Jones (9)
St Francis Catholic Academy, Bedworth

The Lost Spy

I awake on each morning
To start a new
Day but today was different
I found myself on the
Streets of America

I was lost where
Did you go? You
Left me here alone
Come back for me
I miss you.

Every night I cry myself
To sleep every
Night but it was
Different

I got a new job
I'm a spy with my friend
One day, she died. I murdered
The killer, I became strong that day.

Isabella Pugh (9)
St Francis Catholic Academy, Bedworth

Cotton Candy Clouds

In a world made of sweet treats,
Everything in this land you can eat.
It is a wonderful sight,
Mud made of Turkish delight.

Clouds of cotton candy,
Trees of liquorice, and jelly drops for grass
Skies of the green-coloured jelly bean
Flowers of all different colours.

And people as jelly babies,
Houses of strawberry laces,
Same with the doors.
The sky is painted with blue raspberry laces,
And the sun a Haribo egg.

Lilith Franklin-Weeks (9)
St Francis Catholic Academy, Bedworth

Getting More Scared

In my dream every night,
A gymnast is teaching me,
I tell her the wrong answer
And she disappears into a different world,
Because I'm bad.
There is screaming and shouting
In the woods.
Crash and bang, it's hard to hear anything.
Then it's two days later
And a new year,
Hopefully, I'll go back to my own world with my unicorn,
Playing football.
I'll miss it here.

Tanyi Okpu (8)
St Francis Catholic Academy, Bedworth

The Right Shaped Ball

I'm lacing up my boots and putting my gum shield in,
With butterflies in my belly waiting for the game to begin.
The stadium is so big, full of people cheering for us to win.
I stand on the line, and as the whistle blows, the adrenaline kicks in.
I catch the ball in the shape of an egg,
And my dream of playing for England becomes real in my head.

Henry Cowan (9)
St Francis Catholic Academy, Bedworth

Dreams

D reams are full of fantasies.
R eal things could happen like being a pirate sailing the seven seas.
E nter the world of dreams so bright, but just not in pure daylight.
A n adventure could happen at night.
M ake the most when you dream even if it is bad.
S o what is the best dream you have had?

Olivia Wigmore (8)
St Francis Catholic Academy, Bedworth

The Dream Landy Of Unicorns

U nder you is a land of unicorns
N ew worlds are full of dreams and hope
I can see the magic
C otton Candy Landy
O n the clouds it is sunny
R ainbows shine which means my friends are here
N ext my magical friend came
S oon we got back to eating cotton candy.

Lucy Packer (8)
St Francis Catholic Academy, Bedworth

Wizard's Poem

I had a dream about wizards doing magic,
And what I am about to tell you next is very tragic.
Everyone would swirl their wands in the air,
And most of the time, the lights would sparkle like in the funfair.

If you use your spell wrong,
You won't become as powerful and strong.
These were the words that the teacher said,
And all of the wizards' faces turned red.

All of a sudden, there appeared a creature,
Making everyone terrified, even the teacher.
It had a huge, round face,
With everyone in the room getting chased.

Luckily for me, I have woken up from that dream!

Serin Durna (10)
St Mary's Catholic Primary School, Loughborough

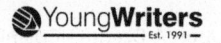

The Disappearing Shadow

My eyes dart open as I look around,
The space where I am unnaturally has no sound,
A place with caves that shine in the night,
And me, who is present, is bathed in moonlight.

The floor shakes and starts to growl,
As my shadow behind me seems to prowl.
"Is this a dream?" I wonder. "I don't know!"
But then my shadow starts crouching low.

It disappears from the human eye,
A scuttling sound as it goes by,
I follow the noise to other caves,
In front of me lie three different ways.

My face goes pale, and my eyes widen;
Which way to go? I can't decide!
I choose the middle - the second way,
Which takes me to a place as clear as day.

Three birds greet me with their names.
Then I tell them of my aims,
Of how my shadow seemed to disappear,
How I followed, and it led me here.

"I've seen a shadow," one replies,
"Though barely visible to my eyes.
It crept along the fields there,
And disappeared, I don't know where!"

"Oh, thank you!" I cry with glee,
"But one more thing before I leave,
You know this place like the back of your hand,
So, can you tell me where I am?"

They're going to answer when suddenly,
The shadow creeps right behind me!
I try to catch it, but I'm too slow.
The shadow runs as fast as a cheetah does!

I catch my breath as it goes to hide,
But hear it rustle, so I must find
Where it has gone, and where it will go,
For if I run again, I'll be too slow!

I walk behind it, and then I see
The shadow's cornered! Can it be?
I'll catch it, go back and leave,
I stretch my arm so I can reach...

But then I wake up from my deep sleep!
Was what I saw just a dream?

My adventure seemed so real to me,
I'll have to see next time I sleep!

Nayara Gondar Aboo (11)
St Mary's Catholic Primary School, Loughborough

The Dry, Dry Desert

I woke up with a start, embedded with sand,
Was this real life or a wonderland?

Ahead of me, I saw a shrine,
Coated with crystals that looked divine.

I stood up and walked to the place,
With an intrigued look on my face.

I prayed and prayed,
But little did I know, I began to fade.

Now you might say,
Was this a dream? Was it all real?
Or was this all fake, like the flying banana peel?

I woke up in my bed, or so I thought.
But this is all an illusion, that your brain has bought.

Mikael Tristanto (11)
St Mary's Catholic Primary School, Loughborough

The Witchcraft Nightmare

From the moment I lay under my covers,
No one could wake me, not even others,
It was as if I was in a coma,
But then I smelt it, that aroma,
I looked around frantically,
My eyes passed the houses that were covered botanically,
I could feel the pressure of villager's eyes,
And hear the desperate, babyish cries,
"Witch!" cried a woman with long, luscious hair,
The glares soon disappeared into thin air,
Then I heard the rhyme,
That said, I travelled back in time,
The next thing I know,
I'm on display for a show,
They had me tied up to a pole,
And they covered me with coal,
"Burn her, burn her!" they all chanted aloud,
As they gathered around me in a big crowd,
A person stepped in front with a sinister smile,
He lit the hay up as it burned for a while,
My confusion melted away into tears,
But just as the fire was reaching my face,

I woke up from those nightmares,
Oh, what a dreadful place!

Victoria Gladiseva (11)
St Mary's Catholic Primary School, Loughborough

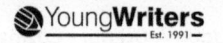

The Sudden In My Dream

What I dream every night
Is to see the stars shining bright
Fairies flying upon me
Leading me to the magical sea
Playing and splashing in the air
Then we go to the enormous funfair
Oh! Dragons and unicorns
Game rooms and candy canes
Suddenly, it rains heavily
Storm thunders and the wind blows
The dragon flies above the roof
And the colourful shooting stars under
The unicorn's hooves
Then the rain stops
The rainbow begins to rise
My dream ends
And I wish it could continue...

Cadee Fung (11)
St Mary's Catholic Primary School, Loughborough

Welcome To Crowstar

Your head hits your pillow as soft as a cloud.
You close your eyes, taking yourself into an infinite pit of darkness.

Bang! You hear noises as loud as a crowd.
"Wow," you say, "feels just like a cloud!"
A voice appears, "Hello, I'm Mary Lou, who are you?"
"I, I..." You try to speak but she has formed a queue.
"I, I can't remember!" you boom.
All of a sudden you are filled with a sense of doom.

Whoosh! You come back to reality, your heart beating faster than a cheetah.

Amelia Farooqi (10)
Trinity All Saints CE Primary School, Bingley

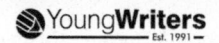

In My Dreams

In my dreams, a music video I was on,
I walked downstairs and on was the song,
On the sofa,
Eating Rice Krispies was an ogre,
I let him be and went to see,
What was in the kitchen,
I thought it was all fiction,
There was a ketchup bottle on the table,
And I wasn't very stable,
Out of it came wizards, unicorns and emojis,
I was going to be late for the music song,
I went upstairs and still the song was on,
I had to dress them in my new expensive clothes,
Then they gave me a pose.

Imogen Shackleton (9)
Trinity All Saints CE Primary School, Bingley

Candy Land Mystery

I wake up in this land,
Then I go for a walk,
When I realise all trees have chocolate trunks,
Cotton candy bushes and leaves.

As I keep on going, I see things move,
They are trolls; although they're rushing,
They are saying "Hurry, we're late!"
Then I follow them.

Soon, in a dreamy castle,
I see a beautiful girl crowned Queen.
Then, *bang!* It is an ogre.
I wake up realising it was a dream!
Or was it...

Amelia Mason (9)
Trinity All Saints CE Primary School, Bingley

Woke Up In A Horror Wonderland

As I woke up, I was introduced to a bubbling lake filled with blood,
I saw half skin-rotted fishes in the lake.
The trees were dead, no leaves left and the bark was as pale as a dead body.
Oddly, there was life, a skeleton dog with a bloody knife.
When I blinked, I was in a small room with flickering light,
An abnormally tall man but no face!
Then I woke up,
Did I die in my nightmare?

Iris Rubery (10)
Trinity All Saints CE Primary School, Bingley

Nightmares!

Welcome to my dreamland centre,
It's not like anyone you'd think of ever,
In my dreams every night,
I sleep very tight,
And the moment I always have to fight,
What I see is crazy clowns,
Creepy sounds,
Nothing has prepared me for this,
Eerie eyes glow,
I close my own in dread,
Suddenly, I wake up to find myself at home in bed!

Aiza Masud (10)
Trinity All Saints CE Primary School, Bingley

Untitled

D o not fear the five eyes
R un from the man who comes at night
E ntirely black and white
A lways stay away from the top eye
M ost wanted is the top right eye...

Erin Irwin (10)
Trinity All Saints CE Primary School, Bingley

The Unicorn Who Speaks

One day, I was walking in Candy Land.
It got closer and closer,
I think it loves me!
Following me all the way home.
Now, it speaks;
Excited, I screamed.
It was a rainbow!

Emily Parker (9)
Trinity All Saints CE Primary School, Bingley

YOUNG WRITERS INFORMATION

We hope you have enjoyed reading this book – and that you will continue to in the coming years.

If you're a young writer who enjoys reading and creative writing, or the parent of an enthusiastic poet or story writer, do visit our website **www.youngwriters.co.uk**. Here you will find free competitions, workshops and games, as well as recommended reads, a poetry glossary and our blog.

If you would like to order further copies of this book, or any of our other titles, then please give us a call or visit **www.youngwriters.co.uk**.

Young Writers
Remus House
Coltsfoot Drive
Peterborough
PE2 9BF
(01733) 890066
info@youngwriters.co.uk

YoungWritersUK   YoungWritersCW
youngwriterscw   youngwriterscw